Tom Longboat

Bruce Kidd

Fitzhenry & Whiteside

Contents

THE CANADIANS®
A Continuing Series

Tom Longboat
Author: Bruce Kidd
Cover Illustration: John Mardon
Design: KerryDesigns

THE CANADIANS® *is a registered trademark of Fitzhenry & Whiteside Limited.*

Fitzhenry & Whiteside acknowledges with thanks the Canada Council for the Arts, the Government of Canada through its Book Publishing Industry Development Program, and the Ontario Arts Council for their support of our publishing program.

National Library of Canada Cataloguing in Publication
Kidd, Bruce, 1943-
Tom Longboat / Bruce Kidd. -- Rev. ed.
(The Canadians)
Includes index.
ISBN 1-55041-838-6
1. Longboat, Tom, 1887-1949--Juvenile literature. 2. Runners
(Sports)--Canada--Biography--Juvenile literature. 3. Indian
athletes--Canada--Biography--Juvenile literature. I. Title. II. Series: Canadians.

GV697.L66K54 2003   j796.42'4'092   C2003-903423-2

Revised Edition
Printed and bound in Canada.
ISBN 1-5541-838-6

© 2004 Fitzhenry & Whiteside Limited
195 Allstate Parkway, Markham, Ontario L3R 4T8

For Jack and Joan, who've been there

Chapter 1
"Finest Made Men in the World"

One hundred years ago, in the early days of Canadian sport, many of the most outstanding athletes were Aboriginals. Dr. George Beers, the Montreal dentist who established the first standard rules for lacrosse, called them "the finest made men in the world."

Athletic contests took many forms in the last century. It was only in the growing cities and towns that men (and a few women) began to organize sport as we know it today, with uniform rules, records, championships, training drills and sports pages in the newspapers. Most people lived in isolated rural settlements, struggling with the soil, the weather, the bugs and the banks to grow enough food to live on. They were only able to get together infrequently, so they usually held their games in conjunction with other community events, such as barn raisings and holidays. The more energetic men also staged athletic contests in the hundreds of mining, logging and railway camps in the hinterland. These were usually tests of strength or one-on-one challenges, accompanied by frenzied wagering. The Aboriginals competed in all these settings. They were increasingly outnumbered by non-Aboriginals, and outside the reserve they rarely took part in organizing contests. But they were always the ones to beat.

The footrace was the most common sporting event in the 1850s and 1860s. Every field day and holiday picnic had its program of races, from 100 metres to several kilometres. In major races cash prizes as large as $100 (in Confederation year that equalled the annual salary of a schoolteacher) would be offered by the organizers. Wherever these races were held, Aboriginal runners were favourites, and usually the winners. Sometimes they were so good they were not allowed to compete in the regular races, but were paid to provide special exhibitions.

Perhaps the greatest runner of the entire nineteenth century was the Seneca, Higasadini, or Deerfoot as he later called himself, from the Cattaraugus Reservation near Buffalo, New York. In the 1850s and 1860s Deerfoot travelled throughout Canada and the United States, challenging anyone to race him for stakes of $250 and giving exhibitions against other native runners. Once, in Hamilton, Deerfoot and his partner Steep Rock won $1000 by outracing three horses in a ten-mile [16 km] relay race. In 1861 Deerfoot travelled to England to race against the best English professionals, pitting his moccasins against their tailor-made spiked shoes. He was rarely defeated. At the end of his tour in 1863, he established a record for the one-hour run (18.3 kilometres) that lasted until British marathon champion Jim Peters increased it by 14.4 metres in 1953, ninety years later!

Footracing continued over the winter on snowshoes. Not surprisingly, the native people, who had invented the shoes, won most of the races. Their exploits were so well known that whenever Aboriginal athletes went on barnstorming tours, they were expected to bring their snowshoes. In the summer of 1867 a team of Caughnawagas gave a snowshoeing exhibition to a blue-ribbon audience in England—over the manicured lawns of Crystal Palace. In Canada, Aboriginal women occasionally put on snowshoe exhibitions as well.

It is often supposed that European settlement of North America quickly drove the Aboriginal people into an isolated reserve existence, where their traditional methods of hunting and fishing became so unproductive that many of them became dependent upon government welfare. But the marginal and often demoralized existence of reserve Aboriginals today is largely a phenomenon of the twentieth century. Prior to World War I many Aboriginal communities were prosperous, industrious and almost indistinguishable from the non-Aboriginal communities in whose midst they lived.

Certainly, the European advance created great difficulties for the Aboriginal people. Strange diseases such as smallpox and syphilis, for which the medicine men had no ready cures, ravaged tribes across North America. Alcohol and the spread of firearms brought death and misery to many others. The

"Finest Made Men In the World"

Christian belief in individual sin and the fur traders' insistence upon trading with individual Aboriginals weakened kinship ties and traditions of community responsibility. But many were able to resist the European culture for long periods of time and to adapt to the problems and possibilities this foreign presence brought to North America.

By the nineteenth century many Aboriginal people had found work among the settlers and traders without forsaking their own language, religion and culture. In the fur trade they not only trapped, but also worked as voyageurs, boatmen, pilots and post employees all along the elaborate transportation networks developed to ship the furs to Europe. (Later in the century the railroad would replace virtually all this native labour.) In the lumber trade they worked as loggers, donkeymen, sawyers and foremen, and individual Aboriginal businessmen (or entrepreneurs acting in the name of a tribe) owned their own sawmills, steamtugs, wharves and trading companies. In eastern and central Canada Aboriginal people farmed their own lands, worked as migrant wage-labourers in nearby farms and canneries and were prominent members of local agricultural societies and women's institutes. In western Canada they worked as cowboys, miners and fishermen. A few became highly educated and made careers for themselves in the professions.

This group of Aboriginal people worked in the nineteenth-century lumber trade at Cape Croker on Georgian Bay

It was because Aboriginal people worked beside so many non-Aboriginals that they were in a position to compete in frequent sporting contests. One reason why the Caughnawaga were widely known as athletes is that they worked—and competed—in so many places. They lived within walking distance of Montreal; many worked as voyageurs and river pilots in various parts of Canada; and after 1882, when they worked on the construction of the main CPR bridge crossing the St. Lawrence, they began to travel all over Canada and the United

Six Nations lacrosse team, 1867

States to do structural steel work for the Dominion Bridge Company.

An important training ground for the Aboriginals' physical prowess was the game of lacrosse. Different tribes had different names for it—"Tewaarathon" among the Mohawk, "Bagataway" among the Ojibway. French missionaries gave the game its present name because it closely resembled an old French game called *la soule*, played with a *crosse* similar to the native stick. Mohawk legend has it that the game was given to humans by the Creator to be played for their and his amusement. People took out their sticks as soon as the snow melted in the spring and played it whenever they got a chance, often for hours on end. Girls and women played too. It was also used as part of religious ritual, to offer thanks to the Creator and to honour esteemed members of the community.

Players trained for major games, strengthening their legs by running with weighted moccasins and practising shots and passes. They kept a strict diet. Rabbit meat was avoided because it was believed to make a player timid, frog meat because it made bones brittle. Many players, like many athletes today, avoided sex before important matches. Despite this systematic training, Europeans came to believe that Aboriginal athletes never trained but excelled on the basis of some "natural" attributes they enjoyed at birth. George Beers was one who romanticized the Aboriginal player in this way. Although he recognized lacrosse as "a means of quickening and strengthening the body," he was convinced the Aboriginals had a "natural" advantage that had to be "gained on the part of the paleface, by a gradual course of practice and training."

After George Beers formed the National Lacrosse Association in 1867, Aboriginal teams began to play under the new standardized rules. They continued to excel, and a team from Caughnawaga won the first Dominion championship. In

"Finest Made Men In the World"

1868 a team from the Mohawk reserve at Akwesasne (St. Regis), about ninety-six kilometres upstream from Montreal, won the championship in a twelve-team tournament in Paris, Ontario. In the next twelve years Aboriginal teams won the title another four times and toured widely in the United States and the British Isles. But in 1880 the newly created Amateur Lacrosse Association declared all Aboriginals "professionals" and banned them from all championship play. The best teams were restricted to an annual Aboriginal championship, held every summer at Caughnawaga before packed crowds and a large brass band. However, Aboriginal teams continued to play against non-Aboriginals in exhibition games, and several non-Aboriginal teams recruited "ringers," Aboriginal players in disguise. (The easiest disguise was a bushy mustache, because it was widely believed that Aboriginals could not grow facial hair.)

Montreal Snowshoe Club

The restrictions on Aboriginal athletes were not limited to lacrosse. In 1873 in Montreal a crowd physically tried to stop two Aboriginal runners from entering the two-mile [3.2 km] open race at the Maple Leaf Snowshoe Club's competition. The two men, Keraronwe and Peter Thomas, were eventually allowed to compete, but when they came home first and second, the crowd tried to stop them from finishing and their victory was hotly protested. Ten days later club officials upheld their win, but subsequently the open race was advertised as "Indians excepted."

These racist restrictions were partly the result of class prejudice. In the early days of organized sport, the soldiers, merchants and lawyers who drew up the rules wanted to compete only against men they regarded as social equals. They invented the amateur code to exclude working-class men from their competitions, declaring all men who worked for a wage in their daily jobs as "professionals" and ineligible. It was for this reason that some of the best Irish lacrosse players in Montreal in the 1880s were declared "professionals" as well. It was only when the growing urban populations created a regular market for sports spectacles and players began to be paid for playing that the definition of "professional" was changed to mean athletes who earned money in sport.

But the restrictions against Aboriginal athletes stemmed from a more complex set of beliefs. On the one hand, these people were regarded as "natural" athletes and therefore unfair competitors. On the other hand, they were considered savages, which made them unfit for competition against civilized men. This second form of prejudice seems to have been on the increase in the 1880s and 1890s. Much earlier in the century, when Aboriginals were staunch allies against the Americans and Fenians and played such a valuable role in the fur and timber trades, they were highly regarded, although racist attitudes were never absent. Throughout the colonial period the British government in London tried to enforce the principle that Aboriginal people enjoyed a claim to the land they hunted, fished and farmed and to involve them in all discussions about their future. But as the military threat receded and the immigrant population rapidly outgrew the available farmland, settlers and their local governments increasingly sought to shunt these same people aside.

Between 1871 and 1923 the federal government forced many tribes to sign treaties, which condemned them to marginal land or "reserves." Whether it was spread consciously or not, the attitude that Aboriginals were inferior, unwilling and unable to learn "civilized ways" provided the justification for pushing them off their land onto reserves. The refusal by Aboriginal tribes to embrace European culture was interpreted as a sign of inferiority. It is only very recently that a Canadian historian, E. Palmer Patterson II, could put these "failures to learn" in a more positive light and suggest that "the Indians preferred to retain as much as possible of their aboriginal culture because they were of the opinion that many of its values were preferable to those of the white man."

Prejudice faced the Aboriginal athlete whenever he competed—if he was not resented because he was too good, he was despised because he was inferior. Racist attitudes were always close to the surface and remain so to the present day.

Eventually, however, prohibitions against Aboriginal athletes were dropped. By the turn of the century such restrictions were less necessary to make certain that non-Aboriginals won in sport. The Canadian population had grown dramatically, especially with the immigration of the 1890s, while the Aboriginal section of the population increased very slowly. As a result, the group from which the immigrant sports clubs could draw was much larger. A much higher percentage of the non-Aboriginal population now lived in cities, where they could take advantage of special sports clubs and the facilities they offered, such as lighted playing fields and indoor gymnasiums. As the competitive side of sport began to take on more importance than its social side, men began to train regularly and systematically.

At the same time, this was a period of gradual economic decline for many Aboriginal communities, when men and women had less time and fewer resources to devote to sport. With the growth of team games such as hockey and football, Canadian sport began to lose its vital connection to the "life" skills in which Aboriginal athletes excelled. So while the 1890s and 1900s were years of tremendous growth in sport for most Canadians, they marked the beginning of a slow decline for Aboriginal sport.

Yet in this twilight period, a man emerged who was to become as famous in his day as any athlete who has ever lived in Canada. His name was Cogwagee, which means, "Everything." His English name was Tom Longboat.

Chapter 2
"Longboat Always Wins"

The Six Nations Reserve lies in gently rolling farm country on the west bank of the Grand River near Brantford, Ontario. George III gave the land (which the British government purchased in 1784 from the Mississauga Indians) to the six tribes of the Iroquois Confederacy as a reward for their loyalty during the American Revolution. At one time it included all the land for ten kilometres on both sides of the Grand from Lake Erie to the forks at Conestoga, but gifts, land sales and the invasions of squatters in the nineteenth century reduced it to its present size, about one-tenth of the original grant. If you drive into Ohsweken, the main village of the reserve, people can still direct you to the site of the log house where Tom Longboat was born on June 4, 1887.

Longboat was an Onondaga. The Onondaga played the leading role in the complex Iroquois system of government, for as "keepers of the fire," they alone had the right to convene council meetings and introduce items of business. Although there were some prosperous Onondaga, Longboat's parents were very poor, and the whole family had to work extremely hard on their small farm. They had a cow, a few chickens and some rabbits, but often they did not have a horse, which meant that the heavy work of ploughing, harvesting and clearing the bush had to be done by hand. Longboat's father died when Tom was five years old. Although he attended the band school three kilometres away, he often stayed home for long periods to help his mother.

But it was not all work—in the winter he loved to snowshoe, and in the summer he would sneak away from his chores to play lacrosse. He was a very agile player, and many people thought he might become a professional. When he stayed away too long, his mother would send his older brother after him, and the chase would go on for hours, ranging all over the

Mohawk Institute,
Brantford, Ontario

reserve and sometimes beyond to the nearby towns of Caledonia and Hagersville. Young Tom liked to fish, too, and whenever they had a chance, he and his brother would run up the River Road, past Caledonia, to their favourite spot. On a good day there would be a fish fry for supper.

About the time of his twelfth birthday, Longboat finished grade four and was allowed to enroll in the Mohawk Institute, an Anglican mission boarding school in Brantford. After schooling at the Institute, some students went on to prominent careers in Canadian society. Perhaps the best known of these was Pauline Johnson, the teacher and poet. But the Institute became a nightmare for Longboat. Though his house was only a few kilometres away, he felt captive in a foreign country. All his fellow students were Aboriginals, but the teachers forced them to speak English. Tom had spoken Onondaga at home and in the band school, and this new language made him feel even stranger. The teachers also tried to persuade Tom to drop his longhouse religion and embrace Christianity. Most of all, he resented having to work each afternoon in the mission's fields. For young Longboat this merely meant that he was weeding and picking for the Anglicans instead of his mother. And unlike his mother, the Anglicans supervised his work very strictly; he couldn't take off for a run or go fishing whenever he wanted.

Pauline Johnson, the Mohawk poet

So the next spring, the first chance he got, Tom ran away. The teachers quickly caught and punished him. But before long, Tom got a second chance and made it to the home of an uncle. His uncle agreed to hide the boy if Tom would work for him. So, at the age of twelve, Longboat's formal education came to an end. He would always remember the Mohawk Institute with great bitterness, and according to his sons, it was one topic guaranteed to rouse his anger. After he became famous, he was invited to return and speak there, but he refused.

During the next few years Longboat worked as a farm labourer, sometimes living at the farms where he worked, sometimes at home, sometimes walking to seasonal jobs in canneries as far away as Burlington. It was during these travels that he discovered competitive running. Almost all the neighbouring agricultural towns had annual field days or Highland Games, with cups, ribbons and merchandise prizes offered in a variety of events. In Brantford and Hamilton there were road races every year, and Longboat was an interested spectator. One of the most prominent runners was Bill Davis, a Mohawk from Ohsweken. Davis had raced successfully all over southern Ontario, and in 1901 he travelled to the Boston Marathon with a group of Hamilton runners and finished second. The veteran athlete regaled Longboat with stories of his races and travels.

In the spring of 1905, just before his eighteenth birthday, Longboat entered the annual Victoria Day five-mile [8 km] race in nearby Caledonia. Longboat started off with a great sprint, and by the halfway point had built up a big lead. But about six kilometres into the race he suddenly began to tire, and another runner, whose name has not been preserved, passed him in the last kilometre. Longboat just managed to hold on for second. During the eight-kilometre walk home— after he recovered his breath and collected a small prize—he

Hamilton was already a booming industrial town at the turn of the century

realized how much he had enjoyed the race, and he vowed to train to get stronger.

Whether Longboat's idea of training came from Bill Davis, from the traditional Iroquois approach to lacrosse or simply from intuition is not clear. But from the beginning he seems to have trained systematically. He began by gradually extending his distances (sport scientists now call this the principle of progression), first using the measured concession roads on the reserve and then running to neighbouring towns.

At first his mother refused to believe him when he told her where he had been running. Once, after he returned from running and walking to Dunnville and back, a total of eighty-three kilometres, she told him she would throw him out of the house if he ever lied to her again. A month later, when his brother was driving a horse and buggy to Hamilton, Longboat waited half an hour and then beat the buggy to Hamilton. That silenced the family skeptics.

Longboat also understood the principle of proper recovery, of permitting yourself to rest after hard workouts so you can bounce back stronger than you were before. For this reason,

Bill Sherring wins the 1906 Olympic International Marathon in Athens

modern athletes usually alternate their difficult or exhausting training sessions with easy or moderate sessions. After his hard workouts Longboat confined himself to walking and sometimes rested completely until he felt ready to run again.

By the time the Victoria Day race at Caledonia came around the following year, Longboat was ready. He took the lead at the starting gun and was never headed. He won by more than four hundred metres.

Longboat worked on a farm during the summer of 1906, but stayed in touch with Bill Davis, who encouraged him to keep training and to enter the annual Hamilton *Herald* race in October, after his farm work was finished. Longboat did just that, and although the chores prevented him from running as often as he wished, the work kept him lean and fit.

Hamilton, a booming industrial town whose steel mills had rolled out the rails for most of the country's railroads, was the centre of Canadian road racing at the turn of the century. In 1900 three Hamilton runners—Jim Caffery, Bill Sherring and Frank Hughson—were the first Canadians to enter the Boston Marathon, and they finished one-two-three. The following year Caffery, a twenty-four-year-old carpenter, repeated his victory at Boston and covered the same course ten minutes faster, with Bill Davis coming in second. Sherring achieved perhaps a more magnificent triumph by winning the marathon in the 1906 Olympic International Games in Athens, Greece.

The most important race in the Hamilton area was the annual "Around the Bay," a 30.5-km course that wound through the industrial area in the east end of the city, over the sand dunes that enclose the bay at Burlington, then back into the city by way of the Botanical Gardens and Dundurn Castle. The race started and finished in front of the offices of the *Herald* newspaper, which had inaugurated the race in 1894.

This course had been the scene of great battles in the past between Caffery, Sherring, Davis and other outstanding runners. In 1906 the favourite, since Bill Sherring had retired from amateur racing to cash in on his new-found fame, was John Marsh, an Englishman who ran for the Telegram Amateur Athletic Club in Winnipeg. Marsh had set several English records before emigrating to Canada.

When Longboat lined up for the start, most of the runners, coaches, reporters and spectators had never heard of him. Although he looked extremely athletic—176 cm and just over sixty kilograms, with long, lean legs—he did not appear to be an experienced competitor. He was dressed in a loose sweatshirt, a threadbare bathing suit and cheap canvas shoes. The local oddsmakers, who were taking bets on the twenty-seven-man field, listed him at 100–1. When the gun went off, he gave little indication that the odds were wrong. Although he sprinted out and quickly tucked in behind Marsh, who took the early lead, he ran with an unusually low stride and held his hands at his hips, well below what was customary for runners of the day.

Marsh kept up his pace, and so did Longboat. By the time they reached the causeway at Burlington, all the other runners had dropped back. They were now running into a stiff breeze, and although he looked like a novice, Longboat was letting Marsh break the wind for him like an accomplished veteran. Every so often he would sprint into the lead for a hundred metres or so—he seemed to have energy to burn! Kilometre after kilometre, the two competitors ran together step for step. If Marsh was perturbed by his unexpected rival, he didn't show it. In fact, each time he resumed the lead after one of Longboat's brief bursts, he smiled confidently to himself.

There is a point in the Bay race where even the best runners are tempted to slow down and coast a bit. It comes just as you turn along Stone Road, after the long climb up from Burlington Beach. There are about six and a half kilometres left in the race, and you want to save yourself for a strong finish. So you take advantage of the flat and the shelter from the wind, and you let up a little.

This is just what John Marsh did in 1906, but it was a terrible mistake. In the instant he slowed, Longboat exploded with speed and left the Englishman as if he were standing still. Marsh was so shocked by the sudden burst that he had nothing to give in pursuit, and within a kilometre Longboat had opened up a lead of two hundred metres. From that point on, despite a steep hill and almost two kilometres of badly rutted road, Longboat ran freely, with a stride that suggested he was out sightseeing instead of running away from many of the best runners in Canada. Longboat finished almost three minutes ahead in 1.49:25. It was only his third race, at a distance four times what he had run competitively before! Bill Sherring may have been slightly relieved to be on the sidelines. "Longboat's gait is not very pretty," he told reporters, "but he is powerful, has speed, and will make a great runner!"

Montreal can lay claim to the title of the "cradle of Canadian sport," because it was Montrealers such as George Beers who first drew up standard rules for lacrosse, rugby football and hockey and who organized the first national governing bodies in many sports. But by the turn of the century Toronto had begun to challenge Montreal as a sporting centre. By the mid 1890s the Ontario city could boast fifty athletic clubs, and a growing list of national sports associations were establishing offices there.

Many Toronto athletes came from families of high social standing. The Toronto Athletic Club, founded in 1891, was housed in a large, luxurious building on College Street (now part of the Ontario College of Art) and counted financier John Massey, railway magnate E.B. Osler, former Ontario lieutenant governor John Robinson and University of Toronto professor Goldwin Smith on its board of directors. But working-class sport had its patrons too. John Ward, a tailor and ardent socialist who worked his way up in politics to the position of city controller, sponsored a trade union baseball league and several races.

One of these was the fifteen-mile [24 km] Ward Marathon. And in 1906, after his Hamilton win, Longboat needed no urging to enter. The race was run over a course that is still popular today, starting at the foot of High Park and running west along Lakeshore Road for seven and a half miles [12 km], then back to the park. The field of seventy-four entries was much larger than in the *Herald* race. For the first time, Longboat was facing runners from the powerful West End YMCA, and this time he couldn't enjoy the advantage of not being known. The bookmakers made him even money. From the start the race seemed to be a copy of the Around the Bay, except it was Longboat who took the lead and Bill Cumming of the West End Y who doggedly hung on his heels. These two gradually left the rest of the field out of sight.

Cumming was a speedster who usually won with spectacular finishing kicks. Now he was trying the longer distances for the first time. But he had not yet built up his strength, and just as the leading pair turned around the halfway marker, Cumming stopped short and sat down by the side of the road. Later he would drive to the finish with an official. By that point Longboat had established an insurmountable lead, and he won by more than three minutes.

The final race of the Ontario season was (and still is) a ten-miler [16 km] held in Hamilton on Christmas Day. It was a nippy Christmas in 1906,

Tom Longboat early in his running career

and although there was little snow, there were large patches of ice on the road and frozen ruts that could instantly twist an ankle. Bill Cumming shadowed Longboat from the gun, and this time he appeared much stronger than before. When Longboat tried to test his Toronto rival by picking up the pace, Cumming accelerated with him. When Longboat returned to his regular rhythm, Cumming slowed down right on his heels. At one point in the middle of the race, a rig driving beside them capsized on the ice and fell on both runners. They scrambled out from under it as if nothing had happened. Cumming's face was badly scratched, but he never lost a stride.

Eight kilometres. Ten kilometres. Twelve kilometres. Had

Longboat found his match? Would Cumming be able to hang on and then sprint to victory in the final block? The runners were now passing the fourteen-kilometre mark. But just as some spectators started to shout, "Cumming could win this one!" Longboat began his finishing kick, and the race was quickly over. In the final kilometre he opened up a lead of fifty seconds and left Cumming looking like a plodder, not a famous sprinter. Longboat's time of 54:50 set a new course record by more than two minutes. When he crossed the line, his face broke out into a handsome smile, soon to become his trademark throughout Canada.

There was no doubt about his ability. He could win following a pace, he could win while shadowed by a big kicker. In three races in less than three months Longboat had set the entire Ontario distance racing community on its ear. The Toronto *Globe* confirmed his rapid rise in its Boxing Day headline: "Longboat Always Wins."

Chapter 3

The Boston

There is magic in the name of the Boston Marathon, the first marathon ever run on an annual basis. Of the hundreds of marathons now held each year in Canada and the United States, the "Boston" is still the race for distance runners.

The first event to be called a "marathon" was held during the first modern Olympic Games in Athens, Greece, in 1896. The Games were the brainchild of Baron de Coubertin, a French aristocrat. He wanted to stage the first modern games in Greece, the country that gave us the "Olympics" almost three thousand years ago. One of his friends, a Paris schoolmaster named Michel Bréal, suggested that one of the events should be a race to commemorate the legendary run of Phidippides, who ran all the way from the battlefield near the little town of Marathon to Athens to announce the Greek victory over the Persians. When Phidippides entered the city, he shouted, "Rejoice! We have conquered!" and then collapsed and died. The first Olympic "marathon" was run from the site of the ancient battle to the new Olympic Stadium, a distance of about thirty-eight kilometres. It was the final event of the six-day program. When a Greek runner won the new race, the success of de Coubertin's venture was assured.

Several officials from the Boston Athletic Association had journeyed to these Games. They were so captivated by the new event they decided to stage a marathon of their own. The first race was held April 19, 1897. It was a point-to-point course like its model, stretching forty kilometres from the little town of Ashland to the BAA clubhouse in downtown Boston.

It was not long before Canadian runners were attracted to the Boston, for as sport became more and more popular, an increasing number of Canadian and American athletes crossed the border in search of competition. As early as 1844 an

American race promoter had placed an advertisement in the Toronto *Herald* inviting entries in a one-hour run for a first prize of $600. By the 1890s baseball leagues had begun to straddle the border, with several outstanding players, such as Fredericton's Larry McLean, hired by the best American teams.

When the Hamilton contingent first entered the Boston in 1900, betting was largely along nationalist lines. When Caffery won and then repeated in record time the following year, the Boston papers griped, while the Canadians rejoiced. But for several years after, no Canadian had come even close to winning. So in the early months of 1907 one thought was foremost in the minds of Canadian sports enthusiasts—Tom Longboat for the Boston.

A race in February indicated that Longboat was a competitor who would give every ounce of energy in a race. It was a three-mile [4.8 km] match race, one-on-one, between Longboat and George Bonhag of the Irish American Athletic Club of Buffalo, New York, held on Bonhag's home ground in the 74th Regiment Armoury. Bonhag was a remarkable competitor. He was the U.S. five-mile [8 km] champion and held the U.S. indoor three-mile record at 14:44.6. In 1906 he had been favoured to win the five-mile in the Athens International Games, but was outkicked in the final stretch. Bitterly disappointed, he entered the 1500-metre walk, an event in which he had never competed, and won. By the book he should have blown Longboat off the track. Longboat had never approached Bonhag's speed in a race and had never competed indoors. But his fame had spread so widely that 9,000 paid to see the race.

Longboat took the early lead, but couldn't hold it. By the second kilometre the American was running easily in front. Though Longboat appeared to be sprinting full out, losing ground on every turn, he was never more than three metres behind. Three kilometres passed and Bonhag still had not broken contact. With less than a kilometre to go, Longboat not only closed the gap, but moved up on Bonhag's shoulder and challenged him for the lead! The crowd jumped to its feet. Straining with every step, Longboat inched ahead on the short straightaways, only to fall back slightly as they rounded the bends. At the bell lap they were dead even! On the last turn Bonhag managed to get a full stride ahead, and he won by twenty centimetres. Both men broke the American record, with the winning time recorded at 14:43.4. It was a spectacular performance by Longboat, demonstrating speed no one had dreamed of.

But before he could even enter the Boston, Tom Longboat had to weather a challenge to his amateur status. Shortly after the Ward Marathon a Toronto businessman named Harry Rosenthal had travelled to Ohsweken and offered to be Longboat's manager.

Longboat would continue to train on his own, but Rosenthal would handle the details of filing entries, arranging transportation and trying to get expense money. He would also help Longboat find a job and a place to stay in Toronto. Rosenthal said he wanted no money for his work; he would make money by betting on Longboat.

Longboat was flattered by the offer and readily accepted. He'd always wanted to travel and race in other parts of the world, and he was intrigued by the possibility of living in the big city. Bill Davis had warned him about promoters who exploited Aboriginal athletes, but Davis didn't have the time to be manager himself, and Longboat thought he'd take his chances.

At first the arrangement worked out fine. Rosenthal entered Longboat in the Hamilton Christmas race and arranged a successful exhibition at Toronto's Dufferin Park Race Track. But when Rosenthal set up the match against Bonhag, track and field officials in both Canada and the United States began to object publicly. They suspected Rosenthal was taking more than legitimate expenses, in violation of the amateur rules. One week before the Bonhag race, Norton H. Crow, secretary of the Canadian Amateur Athletic Union, announced he would not grant Longboat the permit necessary for competition in another country. Only after the

Longboat in his amateur days. When he won the Ward Marathon for the third time, the large silver trophy for the race was awarded permanently to him

captain of the 74th Regiment came to Toronto and swore an affidavit that Longboat was not being paid did Crow relent. After the race, Rosenthal and Longboat were again refused a permit for a match race in New York against another American champion, Frank Nebrick. The CAAU's message was clear—if Longboat wanted to race internationally again, he would have to get another manager.

It was a difficult decision. Although Longboat wasn't entirely satisfied with Rosenthal, the businessman had kept his part of the bargain, including finding him a job with Gage Publishing Company. But Rosenthal wouldn't stand in his way. At the CAAU's direction, Longboat joined and moved into the West End YMCA. After an official investigation, the CAAU cleared Longboat of taking any money for his race performances. The Y announced that it would enter Longboat in the Boston and that E.B. Osler would donate money for his expenses.

Seven Canadians entered the Boston that year—Longboat, Charles Petch and Harry Kerr from Toronto; Dennis Bennett and Bill Lebarre from Hamilton; Tom Shipman from Montreal; and Gordon Wolfe from Halifax. Their photos were all published in the Boston newspapers. Longboat received the greatest attention, and when he refused to grant pre-race interviews, according to Lou Marsh of the Toronto *Daily Star*, "they just faked up interviews and let it go at that ... One photographer missed Longboat but his enterprising sheet dug up an old cut of an Indian football player and ran it over Tom's name."

On the morning of the race a cold breeze began to blow across the city. It would hit the runners square in the face. The temperature was 4°C and the sky was heavily overcast. Not a forecast to sooth Longboat's cold, nor the nerves of C.H.

Ashley, the YMCA's physical director who had accompanied him to Boston. At nine o'clock 104 runners assembled in front of the BAA clubhouse to drive in cars to Ashland and the start.

The gun was fired at noon sharp. Jim Lee of New York quickly took the lead, immediately followed by a pack of six runners. Longboat was running farther back with Sam Mellors, a previous Boston winner, and the pair of them were quickly falling behind. At nine kilometres Lee held a fifty-metre lead on the pack. Longboat and Mellors were more than a minute behind. Another bunch of runners trailed about one hundred metres behind Longboat and Mellors.

At eleven kilometres Longboat suddenly came to life and picked up the pace, pulling Mellors with him. By sixteen kilometres they joined the pack, but now Lee was one hundred metres in front. Then Longboat accelerated again, and four runners dropped back, leaving Longboat in second with Mellors and Charlie Petch hot on his heels. Lee was still running strongly, but with Longboat breaking the wind, the threesome gradually narrowed the New Yorker's lead. They caught him about one kilometre farther on, and when Lee saw his pursuers running beside him, his shoulders suddenly tightened and he dropped behind. It was now a three-man race. As they passed Wellesley College, a crowd of women sang out, "Tom Longboat, he'll win." Longboat grinned and waved, and the relentless pace continued.

A moment later Mellors was accidentally knocked over by one of the many cyclists who were following the race. Petch instantly took advantage of the fall and broke into a sprint. Longboat matched him stride for stride, and the two Toronto runners were all alone in the lead. Twenty-two kilometres. It began to snow. Twenty-four kilometres. Twenty-six kilometres. Longboat was now pushing the pace again, but Petch was hanging on grimly. They were approaching Newton Hills, about thirteen kilometres from the finish. At the beginning of the second long hill, Petch wobbled slightly. Longboat saw the hesitation and was gone. At the crest of the hill he had a lead of one hundred metres, and as he hit the flat he lengthened out and sprinted for about four hundred metres. The race was all but over.

The crowds began to grow. During the last six kilometres the police had trouble keeping them off the street, and some-

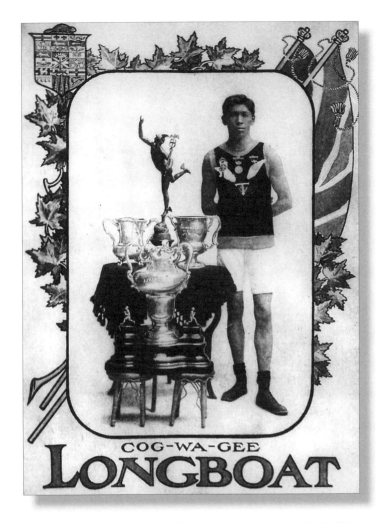

COG-WA-GEE
LONGBOAT

Longboat with his many awards, including the Boston Marathon statue of Mercury

times Longboat had to slow down to avoid collisions. "Everybody knew him from the half-page pictures the papers had published," Lou Marsh wrote, "and they all cheered him ... Tom finished the 25 long, weary miles [40 km] like a good fast miler." His winning time of 2.24:24 broke Caffery's course record by five minutes.

After the race Longboat quickly showered and sat down to "tenderloin steak, chicken broth and numerous other viands" while other runners were still finishing. Then the governor of Massachusetts presented him with a gold medal (for breaking the record) and a bronze statue of Mercury, standing over one metre high. "I knew I could win the race and break the record," Longboat told the press.

In Toronto plans were immediately begun for a gala celebration. City officials sent Longboat a telegram of congratulations and called a special meeting of the reception committee to plan a parade to City Hall. "I don't know anyone who has done more to help the Commissioner of Industries than this man Longboat," Controller Hubbard told the committee. The question was what kind of award to give. "I have been thinking of the silver cabinets, etc., which other runners have received," said Controller Ward, "and I have decided that they are not fitting for this young man who has practically no home but a boarding house." The committee then agreed to give Longboat $500 for his education.

Four days later Longboat and Petch returned to Toronto by train. At Parkdale hundreds of cheering, singing supporters of the West End Y boarded the train for the last leg to Union Station, where they were greeted by thousands of fans and the Highlanders' Band. Two other bands accompanied them up Bay Street to City Hall. On behalf of the city, Mayor Coatsworth presented Longboat with a gold medal and promised $500 for his education. The champion's thanks were modest and quiet spoken: "Mr. Mayor, I thank you kindly for the splendid reception, for the medal and the City grant and I shall try to prove myself worthy of the City's kindness."

But even in this moment of triumph and celebration, few Canadians could see beyond Longboat's label as an "Indian." Few could overcome their prejudices and see him as an individual human being. The Toronto *Daily Star* editorialized:

> *Canada makes no bones about gaining a little glory from an Indian. In other matters than footraces we have become accustomed to leaders from the Six Nations. We give the Boston papers notice, one and all, that we claim Longboat as a Canadian.*

But by "claiming" him and suggesting that as an Aboriginal he was different from other Canadians, the *Star* was confirming the racist practice of treating Aboriginals as inferiors. In fact, the *Star* made Longboat sound more like a racehorse than a human being:

> *His trainers are to be congratulated, not only on having such a docile pupil, but on being able to show such excellent results from their regime. It is to be hoped that Longboat's success will not develop obstinacy on his part and that he will continue to be manageable. If he does not lose his head or begin to break faith with the public, he has other triumphs in store and as much adulation as any mortal man could wish.*

If he was treated this way when he won, how would people respond to Tom Longboat when he lost?

Chapter 4
The Olympic Games

Today, the five interlocking Olympic rings are recognized by more people than any other advertising symbol. In 1976 the Montreal Games were broadcast by 180 radio and television networks around the world. It was perhaps inevitable that the Games would become so popular. They personify the scientific progress, nation state competition and spread of western technology and culture that characterized the twentieth century. But the Games were not always as well known, nor as important. It took several weeks for the sketchiest reports of the 1896 Games to trickle back to Canada. A mere 311 athletes from thirteen countries competed in forty-three events in nine sports, and 230 of these were from Greece. Virtually all paid their own way and entered on their own. The idea of national teams was still very much in the future.

Four years later in Paris the number of entrants increased dramatically to 1,319, but the athletic events were all but forgotten in the much larger Universal Paris Exposition of which they were a part. Pierre de Coubertin feared that the second Games might be the last. The only Canadian entered was George Orton, an outstanding middle-distance runner from the University of Toronto who lived and worked in New York. He competed (and won the steeplechase) as part of the American "team." But forty-one Canadians competed in the 1904 Games in St. Louis and most returned with medals. Although the best English and European athletes were absent (525 of the 617 athletes were American), the Canadian success created a strong interest in Olympic competition. So when it was announced that the 1908 Games would be held in London, England, the capital of the British Empire and the ancestral home of many Canadian sports, the CAAU set up a committee to organize an official Canadian team. The same phenomenon occurred in the other British Dominions and many other countries. For the first time, it looked like the Olympic Games were here to stay.

After his victory in Boston, Longboat was considered a shoo-in for the Canadian team. During the summer of 1907 he continued to look like the man to beat. After a brief holiday at Ohsweken he finally met Frank Nebrick in a three-mile [4.8 km] match race in Toronto and simply ran away from the American champion. In July he won easy races in Toronto and Hamilton and, seeking further competition, ran five miles [8 km] against a relay team in Ottawa, outkicking the final runner and setting an unofficial new Canadian record of 25:55. In August he beat the Irish champion, Joe Daley, over four miles [6.4 km] in Toronto and then narrowly lost to another relay team over three miles in Buffalo. In September he won three races, and in October he recaptured the Ward Marathon, now lengthened to twenty miles [32 km], in 1.41:40, twelve minutes faster than the world record. But since the course had not been measured accurately by a surveyor, his time could not count for a record. The following week, Longboat lowered the Canadian three-mile record to 15:09.6 at Varsity Stadium.

Tom Longboat (second from right) and other runners from the Irish Canadian Athletic Club. At the far left is James Duffy, who won the Boston Marathon in 1914

Longboat ran most of these races in the colours of a new club, the Irish Canadian Athletic Club (ICAC). In July the YMCA had expelled him for breaking curfew, but it was a mutual parting. He never enjoyed the Y—its training rules prohibited alcohol and sex, and its coaches were always preaching to him about discipline and self-reliance. It reminded him of the Anglican boarding school.

The Irish club was more to his liking. It was managed by Tom J. Flanagan, who was an outstanding hammer thrower

Tom Flanagan puts the shot

and as well connected with the Toronto athletic establishment as the men at the Y. But he had a different outlook on sport. As owner of the Grand Hotel in Toronto, Flanagan rejected the temperance creed and never stopped Longboat or any other athlete from enjoying a drink. In an article on training published in the *Evening Telegram*, Flanagan wrote: "I do not advocate ale-swilling, any more than I do overeating, but I do hold that beer will stand by a man and keep him from getting stale and tone him up. To me it is a food and upbuilder." Nor did Flanagan prevent Longboat from enjoying the company of the growing number of women who sought his friendship.

Flanagan differed from the Y leaders in another important respect—he favoured professional sport. As an entrepreneur, he sought to capitalize on sport in whatever way he could—by staging events, by betting on their outcome and by managing professional athletes. Later in his career he would manage Jack Johnson, the heavyweight boxing champion. Although he tried to ensure that the amateur athletes in his club were not suspended for breaking CAAU rules, these rules were not his by choice.

We can only guess at the arrangement Flanagan made with Longboat. He would schedule Longboat's races, give him expense money and keep him clean with the CAAU. Although Longboat did most of his training on the reserve, Flanagan gave him room and board at the Grand Hotel whenever he came to Toronto. In return, Longboat would run in events Flanagan was promoting and wear the colours of the Irish Canadians. The arrangement seemed satisfactory to Longboat, who had left his office job with Gage to concentrate on full-time training. He was now running faster than ever.

But it was one of Flanagan's promotions that cost Longboat his amateur status in the United States. In February he raced—and defeated—three other ICAC runners in a ten-mile [16 km] exhibition in Boston's Park Square Auditorium. The winning time was announced as 50:52.8, a new American record, but the next day the Toronto *Star* reported that several spectators clocking the race had disputed the time. A more serious controversy erupted a week later. The New England AAU, suspecting that Longboat was paid more than expenses (but without a scrap of proof), declared all four runners professionals. The decision would cost Longboat the chance to defend his Boston Marathon title.

In the midst of the controversy, Montreal *Star* publisher Hugh Graham publicly offered Longboat money to stay amateur. His telegram indicates the moral and nationalist expectations placed upon Longboat:

> *Canadians are proud of what you have done in the field of sport ... Your own victories may gratify your personal ambition, but that should not be the end of it. Your country can be not a little served by a continued example of clean sport.*
>
> *If at the end of five years you are still in the athletic field and it can be truthfully said of you that you have resisted temptations, kept temperance and managed yourself always on the side of clean sport, I shall be most pleased to hand you a cheque for $2000.*

Unfortunately, Graham's offer was interpreted by the Americans as further evidence of Longboat's professionalism. But at the Canadian inquiry that followed, Flanagan was able to provide enough statements and receipts to convince the CAAU that Longboat had not broken the rules.

Although he missed the trial for the Olympic team because of a bad attack of boils, Longboat was named to the Canadian team on the basis of his many outstanding performances. Once recovered, he ran an exhibition over the trial course and clocked more than a minute faster than the time of Harry Lawson, the trial winner.

In the weeks before the Olympic race Canadian newspaper readers were treated to almost daily reports of Longboat's training at a special camp in Ireland. "Longboat an Idol, Is Training Faithfully," the Toronto *Daily Star* headlined on July 3. A few days later it reported, "Good luck went up from hundreds of throats as Tom Longboat started on a 14-mile [22.5 km] run from Kilbreedy." Ten days later Lou Marsh reported that Longboat had run seven miles [11 km] in 34:30

Runners race through the streets of London in the 1908 Olympic Marathon

and twenty-one miles [33.8 km] in 1.57. In London his name was kept before the public in an unsuccessful attempt by the American AAU to have him banned from the Games. When he finally arrived in London, crowds followed him everywhere. On the eve of the race the Toronto *Daily Star* front page blared: "Longboat, Fit as a Fiddle, and Idolized by the British Public."

The distance for the 1908 Olympic Marathon had been lengthened to 42.2 kilometres, a decision that many marathoners still rue today. In 1896 the distance was thirty-eight kilometres, and that was lengthened to just under forty-two kilometres at the 1907 Athens International Games. But in 1908 the Royal Family asked that the start be held at Windsor Castle so that Edward VII's grandsons, including the future kings, Edward VIII and George VI, could see it at close range. The shortest distance between the green at Windsor Castle and the Olympic Stadium at Shepherd's Bush was 42.2 kilometres, and that became the new official distance.

Longboat's greatest challenge would come from four English entrants, Duncan, Jack, Lord and Clarke. Although none of them had posted times that came anywhere near Longboat's magnificent record in Boston, they had all run several marathons that spring and had practised frequently over the Olympic course. (Longboat hadn't raced a full marathon since Boston.) Longboat had beaten the most prominent members of the twelve-man American entry, with the exception of Louis Tewanina, a Hopi from Arizona. Twelve Canadians were entered, including Harry Lawson, Fred Simpson and Jim Caffery, now thirty-one. Coach Bill Sherring told the press that Simpson and Lawson would give Longboat a race for the title.

Despite a blazing sun, the frontrunners took off rapidly. Four Englishmen shared the lead, followed by Longboat and three other Canadians. At the one-kilometre mark they ran through two lines of boys from Eton College, who shouted and whistled them on. The adrenaline must have been pumping, for they covered the first mile in a blistering 5:01.

At Slough, six and a half kilometres into the race, with the crowd three and four deep, Tom Jack held a fifty-metre lead on a bunch that included three Englishmen, South African champion Charles Hefferon, Dorando Pietri of Italy and Longboat. The Americans were well behind.

Jack's split was 21:18, an average of just under 5:20 a mile. But the fast pace in the hot, muggy weather was soon to take its toll. At eight kilometres Jack had to stop for a drink, and when he started again, he could only manage a jog. He was the first to drop out.

At fourteen and a half kilometres Lord and Price of England were sharing the lead, with Hefferon, Pietri and Longboat spaced about ten metres apart, eighty to one hundred metres behind. Although the leaders' pace had dropped to six minutes per mile [3.75 min/km], they still held a wide margin over the other entrants.

Between seventeen and eighteen kilometres Price threw in a burst, dropping Lord and widening his margin over Pietri and Longboat. Hefferon was the only one who was able to keep in contact, and the South African soon passed Lord to move into second. The heat and the fast early running continued to take its toll. Now Price began to falter. He was passed by Hefferon at the crest of a long hill and soon joined Jack and Duncan, the other English favourites, on the sidelines. The South African showed no signs of wavering, and by twenty-four kilometres his lead was more than two minutes over Lord, Pietri and Longboat, now running a few metres apart.

At this point Longboat began to make his move. In a few strides he left Pietri and overtook Lord. Although he couldn't make a dent in Hefferon's enormous lead, he was running smoothly and strongly in undisputed possession of second. The Canadian contingent following Longboat on bicycles and in cars started to cheer louder than ever.

Suddenly, Longboat seemed in trouble himself. At twenty-seven kilometres, still in second, he slowed to a walk, and Hefferon increased his lead to three minutes. But when Pietri passed him, Longboat quickly revived and in a few hundred metres recaptured second place and his steady rhythm. Briefly silent, his supporters began to cheer loudly once again. Twenty-nine kilometres. Thirty-one kilometres. They were now passing through Harrow. The Englishman Appleby caught Longboat and briefly challenged him. But Longboat put in a sprint, and

Appleby dropped back as quickly as he had appeared. He, too, would retire from the race. Spectators began to shout that Hefferon was tiring!

Suddenly, just before the thirty-two-kilometre mark, Longboat stopped abruptly and fell to the ground. He staggered to his feet and tried to continue, but medical officials quickly forced him into a nearby car. Longboat was out of the race! His followers were speechless. When the news was flashed to the stadium, the Canadians groaned and squirmed as many in the crowd began to laugh. In Montreal "the crowd faded away without a cheer worthy of the name."

The race was turning into a survival contest. Hefferon held a big lead over Pietri, but he had slowed considerably. It took him 8:22—barely a walk—to complete the twenty-second mile [35.4 km]. At thirty-eight kilometres the South African's lead had wilted to a few metres. This was the last news wired to the 90,000 spectators awaiting the runners in the stadium, and Pietri was soon to pass him.

But Pietri's effort to catch the South African had exhausted him, and when he staggered into the stadium he was almost unconscious. When he reached the cinder track, he turned the wrong way, tried to correct himself and collapsed. The stadium thundered in a wild uproar. Doctors and attendants rushed to his aid and helped him to his feet. He staggered down the back-stretch, but collapsed again at the beginning of the turn, with less than two hundred metres to go. He struggled to his feet without assistance (to thunderous cheering) and tottered around the bend and down the final straight, falling and climbing up again several times. But forty metres from the finish he collapsed again and lay still.

At this point a second runner entered the stadium—not Hefferon, but the American John Hayes! Two officials picked up Pietri by his elbows and escorted him across the line. He was then carried away on a stretcher, while Hayes finished thirty-two seconds behind. Hefferon staggered in third, another forty-eight seconds behind, and he, too, was carried off on a stretcher. The rest of the runners followed about a minute apart. Only twenty-seven runners, fewer than half the field, finished.

There was almost as much excitement after the race as during it. When Pietri was announced the winner, the Americans protested that he should be disqualified for receiving assistance.

Then Hefferon protested that Hayes had received unfair help. When the officials sorted it out Pietri was disqualified and Hayes declared the winner in the time of 2.55:18.4. Hefferon was second. Canadian Bill Wood, Fred Simpson and Harry Lawson were placed fifth, six and seventh.

The post-mortems in the Canadian camp were carried on the front page of Canadian newspapers. "The Canucks are completely puzzled," wired Lou Marsh. "Trainer Bill Sherring merely shakes his head when asked for an explanation. He says that the strange weather conditions might have had something to do with it ... He says that every Canadian on the team can beat the winning time in Canada." The Toronto *Daily Star* attempted to console its readers by pointing out that both Hayes and Hefferon were born in Canada.

Some people suggested that Longboat had over-trained in Ireland. Others, who noted that Flanagan had advised all listeners to bet heavily on Longboat, suggested that he had been drugged to guarantee a betting coup. In this report, team manager J.H. Crocker wrote:

> *All say that Longboat was running well at the twentieth mile [32 km] in second place. He collapsed without warning and complained of a severe pain in his head ... As soon as he was brought in I went over and examined him carefully ... I found a weak pulse—the respiration was very slow—a pinpoint pupil which was not sleep. To all appearances, someone had got anxious and thinking to help the Indian by giving him a stimulant, had given him an overdose.*

Crocker rejected any suggestion that Flanagan had doped Longboat to put him out of the race. Flanagan later explained that "stimulants were only resorted to when Longboat was on the ground bleeding from nose and mouth ... but no power on earth could have made Tom move in his helpless condition."

Longboat was shattered. According to Marsh, "when he regained his senses, he said all he knew was that he was stricken by a sudden weakness and dropped like a log. He is very sick today. He says he has run his last race."

Chapter 5
Champion Of The World

J.H. Crocker advised Longboat to take three months complete rest, but Flanagan persuaded him to tackle a full schedule of races instead. On August 15 he ran an indifferent ten miles [16 km] in Hamilton, barely holding off Fred Simpson. Five days later in a five-mile [8 km] race at the Toronto Police Games, he was unable to fight off his own clubmate, Percy Sellen, and he was sick after the race. Several bystanders were quick to suggest that Tom Longboat was finished. Even Flanagan hinted to the newspapers that "the Indian might be all in."

But if there was any doubt in the public's mind, there was none in Longboat's. In the dressing room after the police games, he told Sellen, "Next time I'll beat your head off!" Three days later, over the same distance at the Hamilton Jockey Club, he did just that, gradually pulling away from Sellen to a twenty-metre victory. Five thousand fans were wild with delight. A week later in Halifax he outkicked Sellen at the Canadian championships, setting a new national record of 26:05.6. He was just as busy during the fall, winning a string of races at weekend fairs throughout southern Ontario and capturing his third straight Ward Marathon title. His margin at the finish was more than eight minutes. After a similarly convincing win in Montreal, CAAU president William Stark commented that "since his return (from the Olympics) he has proven himself the greatest long distance runner of the century."

But Longboat had run his last race as an amateur. He had not been happy during his few stints as an office boy in Toronto, however grateful he was for the weekly wage. The work was inside; the hours were long and the tasks boring. Nor was he happy with his dependency on the expense money Flanagan gave him. Racing professionally would give him the chance to earn money openly—and in large amounts.

The opportunity to turn pro had existed for more than a year in the form of a challenge from the English professional Alfie Shrubb. A former bricklayer, Shrubb had dominated the English amateur scene until he was declared a professional in 1906 for receiving too much expense money during a tour of Australia. As an amateur he had set nine world records, some of which are still competitive today—he ran five miles [8 km] in 24:33.4, and ten miles [16 km] in 50:40.6. When the American AAU claimed that Longboat was a professional, Shrubb challenged him to five races at five, ten, fifteen, twenty and twenty-five miles [40 km] for $1000 a race. Although Longboat immediately turned him down—he was interested in racing Shrubb, he said, but he wanted to remain an amateur for the Olympics—Shrubb repeated the offer at regular intervals.

On the heels of the massive Olympic newspaper coverage, a pair of New York promoters announced a series of indoor matched marathons to be called "the World's Professional Marathon Championship." They had already signed Dorando Pietri to race John Hayes, and they invited Longboat to challenge the winner. The winner of the second race would go against Shrubb. Longboat quickly agreed. When Pietri beat Hayes on November 25 in Madison Square Garden in 2.44:20.4—more than ten minutes faster than Hayes's winning time in London—the stage was set for Longboat to race the Italian on December 15. First prize was $3000. The loser would take home $2000.

As Longboat and Pietri toed the starting line, they presented a striking contrast. Longboat stood a full head above his

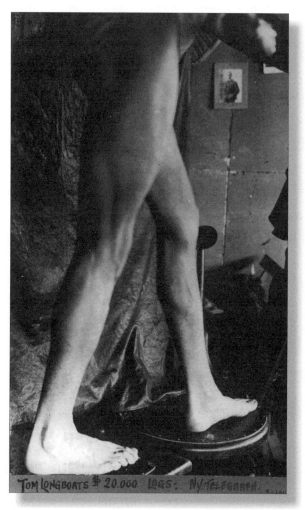

Photo of "Tom Longboat's $20,000 legs" appeared in New York Telegraph

rival. He was well muscled, while Pietri had the classic distance runner's look of skin and bones. Longboat was an outdoor runner, accustomed to rough roads and chilly weather. He was not unfamiliar with indoor running, but the stale, smoky atmosphere made him nauseous. Pietri, in his race against Hayes, had discovered that indoor running was to his liking. His short, nimble stride was ideally suited to the tight turns of the Garden. At ten laps to the mile [6.25/km], 262 laps had to be completed, and the runners would be constantly turning.

At the gun Pietri took the lead, sprinting for the first turn with Longboat hot on his heels. Pietri led through the first mile in 5:14, thirty-three seconds faster than in his match against Hayes. The sellout crowd roared its approval. The brisk pace continued. As the laps ticked away, the differences in the runners' styles become more pronounced.

Pietri, who seemed determined to lead, floated around the track in a constant, unchanging rhythm. Longboat, whose stride was about thirty centimetres longer, moved up on Pietri's shoulder on the straightaways, and then lost ground as he awkwardly made the turns. This constant speeding up and slowing down had to be costing him energy. Longboat occasionally took the lead for a few laps, but Pietri soon became impatient with the change of pace and surged to the front again. It was a fascinating struggle, with neither man showing any sign of weakening. After a quick fifty laps they slowed to six minutes per mile [3.75/km] and held that relentless pace, lap after lap. At fourteen miles [22.5 km] they were seventy-six seconds faster than Pietri's record.

At fifteen miles [24 km] both runners began to tire. The pace dropped suddenly to 6:30 a mile [4:06/km]. At seventeen miles [27 km] Longboat fell back twenty-five metres on a single lap. His effortless stride was gone; he was running mechanically, monotonously, as if in a semi-trance. Pietri took a quick look, and to the delight of the flag-waving Italian section in the crowd, put his head down, determined to widen the gap. But the effort was costly, and he soon began to labour. Although he increased his lead, he couldn't make a complete break.

One and a half kilometres later Longboat appeared to recover and gradually closed the gap. Now it was his turn to make a series of bursts to try to break the race wide open, but Pietri held on. In a few laps Longboat gave up the attempt and settled back into his regular stride. Soon Pietri was back in the lead, with Longboat a step behind. The pace slowed to seven minutes a mile [4.38/km], and both runners looked exhausted. But neither one was prepared to let go.

All of a sudden, Pietri was sprinting again! And this time he didn't stop. Longboat was up on his toes, visibly straining. Just thirty laps remained. The announcer was frantic—Pietri had run the twenty-third mile [37 km] in 6:08 and Longboat was still with him! Twenty-five laps to go and still Pietri struggled to shake the exhausted Longboat. The entire arena was on its feet, hoarsely shouting the men on. Ten laps to go. Nine. Eight. The crowd was almost delirious. Suddenly, both men slowed to almost a walk. Longboat just stayed on the Italian's shoulder, eyeing him warily.

Longboat flashes his famous smile after his indoor marathon victory over Dorando Pietri

But Pietri had run himself out. With just six laps to go he suddenly staggered and collapsed, so unexpectedly that Longboat almost tripped over him. In an instant Tom Longboat was twenty metres, thirty metres, half a lap ahead. Pietri didn't make a move! Just as Longboat was about to lap his opponent, two men ran onto the track and carried Pietri off on a stretcher. The race was over. Longboat finished alone, without changing his speed, in 2.45:05.4.

The news caused a sensation in Toronto. "Longboat Retrieves His Olympic Defeat," the *Globe* proclaimed the following morning, and the accompanying story pushed news of the king's sudden illness off the front page. "Bring on your next champion," the paper gloated. "Longboat is undoubtedly the fastest long distance man in the world."

But before he would race again, Longboat had a marriage to attend—his own. The bride was a Mohawk woman, and her English name was Lauretta Maracle. They were to be married in Toronto on December 28.

In Longboat's day, just as today, the Aboriginal faced many

bewildering contradictions. Some Canadians clung to the outrageous idea that Aboriginals were incurably primitive and used this argument to justify denying them many of the opportunities afforded by Canadian society. At almost the same time as the Toronto city fathers were making a grant towards Longboat's education, the superintendent for Aboriginal education at Brantford, the Rev. R. Ashton, told a public meeting that it was useless to improve the educational standard on the Six Nations Reserve because Aboriginal children could not learn. At the other extreme, many non-Aboriginals believed that Aboriginals could prove intelligent and industrious, but only if they embraced the ways of the dominant culture. These people refused to accept that the Aboriginal could develop his or her own response to the changes in North America brought about by European settlement. There were yet others who romanticized the Aboriginal as the "noble savage" precisely because many of them had resisted European culture.

At the height of his career Longboat had to face all these opinions, but none was stronger than the expectation that he should remake himself in the image of the non-Aboriginal. You'll always be stuck with your native looks, but if you give up your religion and your pride in your tribe, we'll respect you and help you, "civilized" Toronto was saying. The *Globe* made this racist attitude very clear on the eve of his marriage:

> *Interesting a study as the world's champion long distance runner makes—as Indian first and before all—with, over those deep racial attributes, the light veneer of the white man's ways and habits, of far deeper interest is the girl he is about to wed. Here the Indian traits are well covered ... Few would imagine that she had been born and raised on an Indian reservation and was of Indian blood. In every way she is a winsome little girl who has, as she says, been educated away from many of the traditions of her race. She does not like to talk of feathers, war paint or other Indian paraphernalia. She is ambitious for Tom and if anybody can make a reliable man and good citizen of that elusive being, Thomas Longboat, it will be his wife.*

This was subtler than the treatment he received from the Anglicans, but just as racist and cruel.

Although Flanagan, Longboat's best man, forgot the

licence, and the service had to be held up while he raced in a horse-drawn cab to retrieve it, the wedding was a grand success. After the ceremony a gala reception was held in Massey Hall. Montreal *Star* publisher Hugh Graham wired a cash present of $500.

The couple had little time for a honeymoon, however. A return match with Pietri was scheduled for the following Saturday in Buffalo. It was another sellout. Pietri tried to run away from Longboat, covering the first few miles even faster than he had at New York—27:31 for five, 56:30 for ten—but Longboat tucked in behind him and hung on. At eighteen miles [29 km] they were four minutes ahead of their New York time! A few laps later Pietri stepped off the track, completely exhausted. The effort to stay in contact almost vanquished

Lauretta Maracle and Tom Longboat

Longboat as well. As soon as it was clear that the Italian had left the race for good, he stopped and walked several kilometres. His last mile was clocked in 7:38.6 and his final time was 3.03:31.4. Now he had to run the final against Shrubb. The race was set for January 26 at Madison Square Garden.

Few matches in sporting history have received the press buildup of the 1909 Shrubb–Longboat marathon. The newspaper and wire services carried daily accounts and photographs of the runners in training. Special trains were reserved to take spectators from Toronto, Montreal and other Canadian towns. Speculation centred on two questions: Shrubb's strategy and Longboat's condition. The Englishman was the acknowledged master of distance up to twelve miles [19 km], but he rarely raced more than fifteen [24 km] and had never run beyond twenty [32 km]. He planned to run away from Longboat in the early stages of the race, then conserve his strength and hold on to win. However, Longboat was confident: "Shrubb will never finish!"

But if Longboat was to outlast Shrubb, he had to be in contention, and rumours began to circulate about his physical condition. If three races in six weeks had led to Pietri's early

Alf Shrubb stops to change shoes during his 1909 marathon against Longboat

collapse at Buffalo, what would they do to Longboat? This speculation was given substance when Mike Flanagan (Tom's brother), who had been coaching Longboat, suddenly left the training camp. "I wouldn't take $200 a day to handle that fellow," he told the *Globe*. "He is the most contrary piece of furniture I have ever had anything to do with."

Two weeks later Tom Flanagan quit too, selling Longboat's contract for $2000 to Pat Powers, one of the promoters who had organized the series. "I would give a finger to have him beat Shrubb for Canada's sake," Flanagan told the press, "but I'll not be on the track or have anything to do with him personally. He can win if he is right and I know it, but I am out of the Indian's game for good." The *Globe* added an outrageous racial slur to these attacks: "It is the matter of condition that forms the only element of doubt where Longboat is concerned. He has all the waywardness and lack of responsibility of his race." In the midst of this controversy Shrubb asked for a ten-day postponement because of injury. During the delay Longboat silenced his critics by running a fifteen-mile [24 km] exhibition in 1.24:30 in Washington. The late January betting had favoured Shrubb, but by the afternoon of the race the odds were even.

The starting gun exploded at nine o'clock. Uniformed policemen lined the outside of the track to hold back the standing-room-only crowd of 12,000. In Toronto every available hall was equipped with a telegraph service so thousands of others could hear the results. True to form, Shrubb galloped into an early lead, with Longboat running cautiously at his own pace, falling steadily behind. At eight kilometres he was three laps behind. A sixteen kilometres he had been lapped five times, and by twenty-four kilometres Shrubb had increased his lead to eight laps! Each time the Englishman came up to Longboat's shoulder, he sprinted by to prevent him from tagging along, but the Canadian runner only nodded and kept to his own rhythm. Both men were occasionally accompanied by advisers, who gave them liquids and cheered them on, but neither athlete showed any sign of distress.

At twenty-five kilometres Longboat began to run faster than Shrubb for the first time, and the crowd came alive with excitement. As Longboat moved up on Shrubb's shoulder, the Englishman accelerated. The two of them matched stride for stride, Shrubb still in the lead, for almost two kilometres. Suddenly, Longboat broke away; his fans exploded into cheers. He still had eight laps to catch up, but the chase was on. At thirty-two kilometres he had reduced the margin to six laps. There were ten kilometres remaining. Could he do it? Sections of the crowd were already on their feet.

Shrubb leads Longboat in one of their races at Toronto Island Stadium

Now the pressure was on Shrubb. At thirty-three kilometres he stopped, took a drink and walked for half a lap. When he started again, he seemed to be running faster and confidently waved to his supporters. But the rest had cost him another lap. Longboat was still running smoothly, with long, relaxed strides seemingly oblivious to the screaming crowd. Every time he came up to his rival, he would surge up on his toes and pass him with a great burst of speed, but then slow down to his regular pace.

Lauretta Maracle was now on her feet at the side of the track, clapping, dancing and shouting, "Go, Tom, go! Go, Tom, go!" Suddenly, she was joined by Tom Flanagan, who broke through the police lines and began to lead the Toronto cheers. Soon he had taken off his suit coat, shirt and tie and was running up and down one straightaway in his undershirt, alternately cheering Longboat and taunting Shrubb.

As Longboat picked up another lap, the two men sprinted neck and neck around the track. Now it was Shrubb's supporters who took heart. But the effort seemed to exhaust Shrubb, and he had to walk another lap. At thirty-five kilometres, briefly recovered, Shrubb held Longboat off for two laps while his fans cheered frantically. But then he had to stop and walk again. It was only a matter of time now, for although he had begun to slow down himself, Longboat was still running with authority. He caught Shrubb for the last time at thirty-nine kilometres and raced into the lead to tremendous cheers, while the Englishman tottered off the track. Longboat jogged the last sixteen laps to a standing ovation, "amid the greatest excitement that ever marked a contest in the Garden."

Tom Longboat was Professional Champion of the World!

Chapter 6
Professional Runner

Ned Hanlon, Durnan, Scholes, and Longboat, of Toronto

Almost before the excitement in Madison Square Garden had died down, there was a flurry of announcements by other athletes, managers and promoters that they, too, wanted a shot against Longboat. John Hayes, the Olympic champion, wired from Los Angeles proposing a $10,000 race against himself and Pietri, winner-take-all. From Europe came the news that several leading runners would cross the Atlantic to join in the chase. Aboriginal runners Acoose and Fred Simpson both wanted a crack at the champion. Nor were the offers limited to conventional contests. Chicago marathoner Albert Casey challenged Longboat to a 160-kilometre race for stakes of $10,000. The Cole Brothers circus offered him a job as headliner in their main tent.

It was a propitious time for running promoters. In many parts of North America the economy was booming and personal incomes were growing. Between 1900 and 1910 the dollar volume of Canadian manufacturing more than doubled, and the construction of new railroads, harbours, roads and telegraph and telephone lines added to incomes and improved travel and communication. Urban populations were growing rapidly, and the relative lack of free and readily available

At the height of his career Longboat often participated in official functions at city hall. Here he rides in a parade car with Canadian scullers (standing, left to right) Ned Hanlan, Eddie Durnan and Lou Scholes

recreation facilities strengthened the market for sporting spectacles. The team sport corporation, so dominant today, was in its infancy, and there was still plenty of scope for individual entrepreneurs like Flanagan and Powers.

Longboat would ultimately accept most of these challenges, but first he wanted a rest, a honeymoon and a new manager. Although Flanagan had cheered him on during the race with Shrubb, Longboat would never trust the hotel owner again. After the race Flanagan returned to Toronto several days ahead of Longboat and claimed the victory over Shrubb for his own. "I had no intention of stepping into the arena," he wrote in the *Evening Telegram*, "but when I saw how things were shaping I just had to strip off my coat and go at it ... And we won." Longboat rarely responded to insults. He knew words were no match for a fast finish, and he was confident he could silence critics on the track. But this time his reply was quick and decisive:

> *I do not like the idea of doing all the work and somebody else getting all the credit for winning my victories. Do you think that Flanagan could make me run if I do not want to? I can get along without assistance and if any of these runners want to race me they will have to make arrangements with me, and no one else.*

Longboat was also angered that Flanagan had sold his contract without his permission. Pat Powers had a number of sports interests and had no intention of personally overseeing Longboat's affairs. He wanted to place Longboat under the direction of a New York trainer, Jim DeForest. The contract gave the owner a whopping fifty percent of Longboat's gross earnings and permitted the manager to enter him in any race he wanted. Powers had matched Longboat against Shrubb in a fifteen-mile [24 km] race in Buffalo, slated less than three weeks after the marathon, and was trying to enforce the contract. But Longboat was learning fast. He simply refused to talk to Powers. The rematch with Shrubb had to be cancelled.

But Longboat was too hot a property to be ignored. In the weeks that followed, Powers tried to bring Longboat to terms. First, he sent Flanagan as an intermediary. Longboat was polite but adamant: he was not ready to run. Next, Powers threatened to prevent Longboat from ever racing again. Longboat didn't budge. Finally, Powers travelled to Ottawa to request that the

Department of Indian Affairs intervene and enforce the contract. But although Indian Affairs ruled that the contract was binding, it said it had no intention of intervening. Longboat then announced that he would run only if Powers agreed to deposit $5,000 in his bank account before his next race. That was too much for Powers. He reluctantly cancelled a second major marathon.

Public pressure on Longboat to defend his championship eventually led the two men to an agreement. Powers had arranged a six-man marathon for the New York Polo Grounds on April 3. It would match Shrubb, Hayes, Pietri, Matt Mahoney, the U.S. amateur champion, and Henri St. Yves, a French-born London wine waiter and marathoner who had recently sailed to America. Shrubb agreed to compete if Flanagan was barred from the track. Powers needed Longboat if the race was to be billed as a championship. Although Longboat would have less than two weeks to prepare, he agreed. The terms illustrate how shrewd he had become. Longboat would run if Bill Davis, not DeForest, was hired as trainer and if Powers agreed to sell his contract to someone of Longboat's choosing. Longboat agreed to run for prize money only and waived his appearance fee. In turn, Powers agreed to waive his percentage of Longboat's prize. It was a financial gamble for Longboat, but it promised an escape from the New Yorker's grip.

Despite his lack of preparation, Longboat was the 8–5 favourite as the six runners lined up in a cold drizzle before 40,000 spectators. It was a good race with positions changing many times. Longboat ran among the leaders for sixteen kilometres, slowly faded to fourth and then dropped out at thirty kilometres. Shrubb dropped out ten kilometres further on. The winner and new champion was the unheralded St. Yves.

Although Longboat was unapologetic about his showing ("It makes me tired to hear about my condition. I was in good condition, all right."), many of his supporters were bitter. Lou Marsh of the Toronto *Daily Star*, who had basked in the glory of Longboat's previous victories, now turned on him unmercifully:

> *The greatest factor in his defeat was his swelled head. With his cranium enlarged by several victories, which his common sense should have told him were sheerest luck, he thought he could neglect even the rudimentary rules of training and defeat any man in the world.*

Sometimes Longboat's strongest opponent was the weather. At the 1909 Chicago Marathon he collapsed of sunstroke.

Powers sold Longboat's contract to Sol Mintz of Hamilton for $700. To his chagrin, the native runner soon bounced back. In early May Longboat met Shrubb in Montreal over the Englishman's preferred distance of fifteen miles [24 km]. Shrubb led all the way, but it wasn't the runaway that many expected. In June Lou Marsh apologetically reported that "a whole lot of people who figured that the great Tom Longboat was down and out received a rude shock last night when the lanky Onondaga ran away from (Frank) Nebrick in the last mile of a ten-mile [16 km] race ..."

The rejuvenated Longboat then met Shrubb in a twenty-mile [32 km] race at the Toronto Island Stadium. Shrubb had gained a full four-hundred-metre lap by the eleventh kilometre. Then Longboat held him, and the pair tried to break each other with repeated bursts of speed. After thirteen more kilometres of facing neck and neck, Longboat broke away and gradually closed the one-lap gap. When Longboat was less than two hundred metres behind, Shrubb suddenly stepped off the track, and Longboat continued to victory.

In the years that followed, Longboat continued to run dramatic races. He was no longer invincible, but he was always competitive. Now his races were characterized by careful pacing and frequently, a coolly delivered, blinding finishing kick. Once a crowd-pleaser because he was such a magnificent frontrunner, now he was loved and admired because he was such a battler. In 1910 he matched strides with Pietri until the final straightaway of a twenty-miler [32 km], when the Italian pulled away to a narrow victory. He traded wins with Alfie Shrubb again and again. Although they became fast friends and shook hands warmly after each race, their duels were always barnburners. In between the highly publicized matches, he ran exhibitions throughout Ontario and the eastern United States.

Perhaps it was because Longboat was such a magnificent

athlete that fans and sportswriters sought a "special reason" to explain his losses. Longboat was increasingly troubled by knee and back injuries during these years, but when reporters found his times disappointing, they focused instead on racist accusations of "Indian laziness." Flanagan continued to take the credit for Longboat's victories and to spread the legend that Longboat rarely trained.

Banners from some of Longboat's races

Longboat definitely disliked having a trainer crack the whip, and on several occasions took time off to celebrate a heady victory. But there is no evidence that he refused to train. In fact, he seems to have had a particularly good idea of the type of training he needed. The basis for his endurance was always regular, long-distance walking, usually thirty-two kilometres a day. He also spent an hour each day in vigorous activity, such as lifting light weights or playing handball, which he loved. His running was limited to two long runs at varied speeds each week and frequent time trials. Longboat's training displayed early forms of Long Slow Distance and Fartlek ("speedplay"), which are both considered successful training formulae.

After the second Pietri race Flanagan complained that Longboat refused to train, but after two hard indoor marathons in less than three weeks, he undoubtedly needed a rest. Years later Mintz wrote in the Hamilton *Spectator* that after the second race Longboat's feet were "badly blistered from overwork and ill-fitting shoes." Certainly Shrubb did not hesitate to ask for a postponement when he injured his toe. He told the Toronto *Daily Star*, "I never run unless I feel like it. I know there are many athletes that go out to train when they are not feeling quite well, but they are doing themselves more harm than good." Sound advice still today, and from an Englishman it was accepted without question. But Shrubb didn't have a racist stereotype to live down.

Laziness, however, was not the only charge levelled at Longboat during his professional years. In 1911 he received a suspended sentence for drunkenness in Toronto, and the myth of the "alcoholic" Tom Longboat soon took root. A Montreal *Herald* sportswriter suggested the establishment of a "Society for the Promotion of Temperance and Long Distance Running Among Indians." Years later a *Maclean's* reporter wrote that "tales of his drinking became legendary." Although the "tales" persist to this day, the evidence is weak and unlikely. If this alleged alcoholism means that Longboat was incapacitated by drink, his racing record and subsequent steady employment strongly contradict the legend. If it means that he frequented taverns and liked to share a drink with his friends, then he was no different from many other famous athletes of his era and ours. In England, according to sports historian Peter Lovesey, "No professional runner could earn success without passing most of his evenings in the bar, for this was where the races were hatched, backers found and all the vital news from tracks up and down the country were exchanged." It was much the same in Toronto.

Although Longboat remained a popular hero, these stories quickly soured his relationship with many in the Toronto establishment. His civic "grant" provides an intriguing example. After his Boston triumph city council not only voted him $500 "for his education" but also collected another $250.05 by public subscription. Later that year he asked if the money could be used to build a house for his mother, and the board of control agreed. But when the American AAU began to raise a stink about this money and threatened his amateur status, the city treasurer decided to withhold the grant until after the Olympics. In November 1908, at Flanagan's request, the board of control authorized that the money be paid, but no cheque was issued and no explanation was written into the record. Longboat wrote to request the money the following year, but received no satisfaction. In 1910 he wrote again and was paid $50. In 1911, in response to another request, the city sent $165 to his wife. Finally, in 1912, Longboat hired a lawyer to pursue his claim, and the city paid him the remaining $35.05 from the public donations. But he never received the $500.

Sometime in 1911 or 1912 Longboat bought up his contract and began to arrange his races and exhibitions himself. He ran some of his finest races in this period. In January 1912 he travelled to Scotland, where he gave some exhibitions and ran two prize races against Willie Kohlemainen, the elder brother of the glorious Finn who won the 5,000- and 10,000-metre races in the 1912 Olympics in Stockholm and the marathon in the 1920 Games in Antwerp. In the second of these duels, Longboat turned in his fastest time ever for fifteen miles [24 km]: 1.20:04.4. That summer in Toronto he lowered it again to 1.18:10.4, a new professional world record. Tom Longboat was hardly over the hill.

In his first three seasons as a pro, Longboat grossed $17,000, a considerable sum in a period when teachers earned about $400 a year. Although Longboat had to pay a manager plus expenses, he kept a substantial sum, and he was able to dress and entertain lavishly and buy expensive presents for friends and relatives. He built his mother a small, two-storey mansion on the reserve at Ohsweken. He also invested some of the money, but was much less successful in this venture. He was not really interested in the world of business or real estate and made decisions carelessly.

Longboat spent much of his prize money on fancy clothes and gifts for his friends. He and Lauretta also entertained frequently.

After 1912 the interest in matched distance races gradually faded. The economy had begun to sputter; unemployment was growing and spending money was tight. Fewer people were willing to pay to watch yet another race between Longboat and Shrubb. Runners continued to set up exhibitions and races wherever they could, but the professional running boom was drawing to a close.

Chapter 7
The War Years

Several news stories ran in continuous counterpoint to the accounts of Longboat's career early in this century. In western Canada waves of immigration and the wheat boom led to the creation of two new provinces, Alberta and Saskatchewan. In Ontario Adam Beck struggled to establish a public corporation that could deliver inexpensive hydro-electric power to the growing manufacturing centres. In Europe there was continual talk of war. In October 1908, when Longboat was winning the Ward Marathon for the third time straight, attention centred on the escalating conflicts in the Balkans. "War Threatens Europe, Berlin Treaty Torn Up" read the *Globe's* front-page headline.

Throughout Europe governments were rapidly arming. In 1897 Germany set out to build a fleet equal or superior to the famous British navy. In 1906, in response, the British started to build the dreadnought, a battleship with larger guns and greater speed than ever before. But the Germans only increased their building program once again. Chief among the many interconnected pressures that led to war was the growing competition for colonies and markets. These rivalries fed the spread of patriotism, which led to further competition and the stockpiling of weapons. These sentiments also aroused interest in new international sporting competitions like the Olympic Games.

In Canada, British loyalties and the imperialist interests of Canadian capitalists put pressure on the federal government to step up military spending. In 1909 Lord Strathcona, whose banking, shipping and trading companies conducted business in virtually every corner of the British Empire, donated £500,000 to finance military drill as part of high school physical education. The extent and nature of Canadian military support for the Empire was a matter of long and bitter political debate. In 1912 Robert Borden's Conservative government introduced a bill in the House of Commons that would require Canada to spend $35 million to build three dreadnoughts for the British navy. The Liberal opposition used every parliamentary tactic at its command, including a two-week, twenty-four-hour-a-day filibuster, to delay passage of the bill, which was ultimately defeated by the Liberal majority in the Senate.

There were some efforts to prevent or oppose the war. The British government intervened repeatedly in attempts to bring about a settlement in the Balkans. In 1912 Pierre de Coubertin persuaded other members of the International Olympic Committee to award the 1916 Games to Berlin on the grounds that it might dissuade the

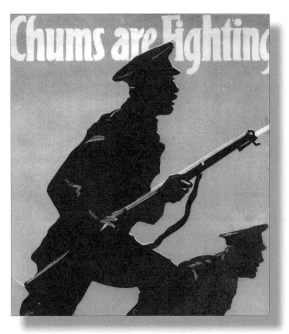

World War I recruitment poster

kaiser from waging war. In Canada trade unions, church groups and many others opposed the Strathcona Trust and the naval bill. In July 1914, just weeks before war was actually declared, socialist groups in Germany conducted large anti-war demonstrations in ninety-one cities and towns.

But when war was declared on August 6, 1914, most people quickly gave in to lurid patriotism and eagerly prepared for the slaughter. Within two months 33,000 Canadian men had enlisted, trained and embarked for England. Volunteer committees quickly formed to prepare food and clothing, medical and recreational supplies and to raise funds. The war effort would bring out the best and the worst in Canadians—heroic sacrifice, ingenuity and bravery as well as incompetence, vicious racial hatred and parasitic profiteering.

World War I had a profound impact on all areas of Canadian life, including sport. In many communities regular sport activities had to be curtailed, or even cancelled. So many athletes enlisted that many teams folded. In 1914 the CAAU cancelled the national track and field championships for the duration of the war. One year later the Canadian Intercollegiate Athletic Union cancelled competition in all sports. The Vancouver Rowing Club, in announcing that it was closing its doors, reported that all but twenty-six of its 187 members had signed up. A few leagues managed to survive, however. In 1916 the Ontario Amateur Lacrosse Association announced that despite the enlistment of two hundred players, more teams than ever before would play in the new season.

Many events were simply taken over by the military, which considered athletic competition an effective way to increase the fitness and morale of the troops. Special units of athletes, or sportsmen's battalions, were recruited across the country. These units formed teams and competed against each other or in existing leagues. Many traditional events, such as the Hamilton Around the Bay race, were restricted to military personnel.

Not all military sports activity was quite so commonplace, however. On April 14, 1915, the Manitoba *Free Press* reported:

> *Canadian troops at the front have discovered a new use for lacrosse sticks, namely throwing of hand grenades into German lines ... Over 500 sticks have been purchased to try out the scheme.*

About 35 percent of the Aboriginal population of military age enlisted voluntarily, a rate slightly higher than the national average. Many bands sent all their eligible members. Aboriginal soldiers were often decorated for bravery. One was Corporal Francis Pegahmagabow from Parry Sound, Ontario, who as a sniper "bears the extraordinary record of having killed 378 of the enemy. At Passchendaele, Pegahmagabow led his company through an engagement with a single casualty and subsequently captured 300 Germans at Mt. Sorrell." Not surprisingly, Aboriginal soldiers were actively recruited and many regiments competed for their services.

The council of the Six Nations at Ohsweken officially refused to join in the war effort. The hereditary chiefs believed that they represented a sovereign nation, allied to the British monarch and not the government of Canada. They steadfastly refused to declare war unless a request for assistance came from London. But unofficially the council lent much support and did not discourage enlistment. A women's group raised money, knit socks, sweaters and mufflers and made bandages. Ultimately, 292 Six Nations warriors went to the front. Among

them was Tom Longboat.

Longboat volunteered in January 1916, during an intensified recruiting drive by the Borden government. Despite the initial confident hopes that the war would be easily won, the end was nowhere in sight. The war had become a savage nightmare for the men on both sides. The initial Canadian commitment of 25,000 troops had proved far inadequate—60,000 "British" troops, including 6,000 Canadians, had been butchered or gassed at Ypres alone—and by January 1, 1916, Borden had raised the Canadian commitment to 500,000.

Longboat's athletic skills and fame made him an extremely attractive recruit. Although he enlisted with the 37th Haldimand Rifles, he soon transferred to the 180th Sportsmen's Battalion. It was not long before he was racing once again, both in competitions and exhibition matches. Even though Longboat was extremely popular in the 180th (and wherever he went), he was transferred from regiment to regiment. In January 1917 he joined the 3rd Reserve Battalion, then doing agricultural work in England, but later that month he was sent

Tom Longboat buys a newspaper from a young boy during a lull in the fighting in France

to France with the 107th, a battalion of Aboriginal soldiers. There he competed regularly in races against other Allied troops. In February he ran third in a large field, beating all other Canadian entrants. In June he won a cross-country race and received "a great reception from his regimental comrades." In August, near Vimy Ridge, he won another cross-country race leading his battalion to the team championship.

In France Longboat served as a dispatch runner, taking messages from post to post. It was difficult and extremely dangerous work. The ground around Vimy and, later, Passchendaele had been torn apart by the constant bombardment and the shifting trench line, and there was mud everywhere. Many of his runs were into trenches where telephone communications had broken down. He had no idea whether there would be Canadians alive to read the messages he carried. It was cross-country running, but with bullets and shells, barbed wire and huge craters. Often the fog would be so thick that he had to stop and wait for it to clear, sometimes sleeping overnight in a soggy field. The wetness made his old back injury worse, and he ran slightly bent over to ease the pain.

Longboat was twice wounded, once declared dead. His death was reported at the front in Belgium. He had just jogged into an officers' communications trench when a shell exploded and buried them. Miraculously, no one was hurt; they were getting air, and they had provisions for several weeks. Since no one was in a hurry to get back under the shelling, they made no effort to dig themselves out until they were "rescued" six days later. "It was the only time I ever got any solid sleep," Longboat later told his son Ted. Like most of his compatriots on active duty, Longboat very quickly tired of the war. Once he was presented to the king, who asked him if there was any favour he could grant. "I'd like to get out of here and go home to see my mother," Longboat replied. But his wish was not granted.

After he was demobilized in 1919 (as a member of still another battalion, the 2nd Canadian Engineers), Longboat ran one more military race in "The Grand Army of Canada Sports Show" at Toronto Island Stadium. Longboat, now thirty-three, demonstrated his classic finishing kick in a three-mile [4.8 km] race against a pre-war rival, Bill Queal of New York. It was now more than ten years since the demise of Tom Longboat had first been predicted.

Chapter 8
"A Perfect Gentleman"

The idealism and patriotism that had persuaded so many men and women to make sacrifices during the war also encouraged them to demand peacetime changes they believed in. During the war, movements for women's suffrage, prohibition, tariff reform, progressive income tax and full employment all gained in strength. Canadian Aboriginals had their own list of demands. The Grand Indian Council of Ontario (which did not include Six Nations) requested that Aboriginals receive the right to vote in return for their many wartime contributions.

Some of these reforms were achieved. The income tax, the vote for women and prohibition (temporarily) were all passed into law. But Aboriginals did not receive the vote until 1960, and many other social goals voiced at the time seem as distant today as they were then. Wartime inflation unleashed an enormous increase in the cost of living, and as the munitions factories and other industries closed down, many soldiers returned to find themselves unemployed and their families hard pressed to eke out a living. It was a time of great hardship and social turmoil.

Tom Longboat was one of the many unemployed veterans after the war. He still ran a few exhibitions, but the days of professional match races were over. He moved west hoping to get a veteran's homestead grant, but ended up travelling from community to community taking whatever work he could get. He now had a growing family to support. In 1918, after he was reported dead, Lauretta Maracle remarried. Although she was delighted to see him alive, she wanted to stay in her new marriage. Longboat soon remarried a Cayuga woman from Six Nations whose English name was Martha Silversmith. They had four children in quick succession. Although he was able to find regular farm work in Alberta, Martha Silversmith wanted to rear the family closer to Ohsweken, so they moved back to Ontario. He worked in the Dunlop rubber plant in Toronto for a year, then moved to Hamilton and eventually on to Buffalo for better-paying jobs in the steel industry. Then in 1926 he was laid off when the growing recession forced a cutback in production.

But in the fall of that year, at the age of forty, Longboat found a permanent job with the streets department of the City of Toronto. He started as a teamster, but when the department changed to trucks a few years later, he became garbageman. It was a position that disappointed the expectations of the sports establishment, and many people regarded him as a failure.

But this inexcusable condescension ignores the hardships created by the economy's regular recessions and permanent unemployment. Longboat may have preferred other work, but jobs were scarce. And with this job he could work outside and walk long distances each day. He never thought of his new position as a comedown and continued to be as sociable as ever. In 1937 the *Globe and Mail* reported:

> *Youngsters in North Toronto are fired with a new ambition, not merely to be engine drivers, G-men or even cowboys. Their growing goal now is to be a street cleaner. That is what their idol is—a man who 30 years ago was the most famous athlete in the world and the idol of Canada ... "Oh, I'm not news any more,"* protested the once famous marathoner when a reporter discovered him sweeping leaves on Lawrence Avenue today. "I've had my day—and no regrets."*
>
> *"You're a pretty important fellow to the children of this district,"* answered the reporter.
>
> *"Well, I'm glad they like me,"* smiled the big Onondaga Indian. "Maybe all I'm good for now is sweeping leaves, but if I can help the kids and show them how to be good runners and how to live a clean life, I'm satisfied."*

The job didn't crimp his style. Throughout the 1930s, when more than a million men and women were out of work and many municipalities went bankrupt because of heavy relief payments, Longboat and his family lived in a comfortable house in a middle-class neighbourhood, ate and dressed well and entertained regularly. Frank Montour, then a professional wrestler and a Six Nations band council member, was a regular visitor. "His house was open for anybody from the reserve and you could expect a good time there."

The family had a car, too. In 1927 Longboat was invited to participate in a special four-mile [6.4 km] race to celebrate Hamilton's Diamond Jubilee. Bill Sherring was entered, as were Eddie Cotter, a former winner of the Bay race, and many other Hamilton favourites. Longboat agreed to enter, on condition that first prize be a secondhand car. He won by fifty metres, "all in the final sprint."

Alf Shrubb and Tom Longboat line up for an exhibition race in 1931

From then on, he often drove his family out of Toronto on weekends, either back to Ohsweken or to various lakes and resort towns in southern Ontario. He took them to hockey, lacrosse and wrestling matches as well.

Each year he officiated at the Bay race in Hamilton, and he usually donated one of the prizes. In all these settings Longboat shook hands, signed autographs and shared his famous smile with everyone. These years were not always happy, however. In 1930, after he had made a guest appearance at the Canadian National Exhibition, his eight-year-old daughter rushed across the street to greet him and was killed by a car.

By 1945 Longboat's back was frequently stiff and sore, so he retired from his job with the city. He worked briefly at an army base in Brantford and as a postman in Buffalo, but he soon retired to the reserve. His fancy house was too big for him, so he sold it and moved down the road. In 1946 he was hospitalized in Sunnybrook Hospital in Toronto with diabetes, but soon went home again. "It was too lonely there," he told

Longboat sold his small mansion and moved into this house on the Six Nations Reserve when he retired

his wife. Despite his ailments, he continued his long walks, and now it was Martha Silversmith who disbelieved the mileage he covered. "He would never thank you for a ride," Frank Montour said. "The last time I saw him it was just after Christmas, and cold. He was walking towards his house and I stopped my car and asked him if he wanted a lift. 'No thanks,' he said. 'Where have you been?' I asked. 'I've just had a nice walk to Hagersville.' That means he must have walked close to thirty-two kilometres that day."

In 1947, after years of silence, Longboat tried to correct the misrepresentations that were part of his "legend." He wrote the Hamilton *Spectator* "to declare war on the cheap two-bit impostor who has been capitalizing on my famous name for the last fifteen to twenty years, by calling himself Tom Longboat for the purpose of obtaining free drinks in various beverage rooms." He enclosed a photo of himself, which showed him as handsome as ever, but with silver-grey hair. Bill Sherring phoned the newspaper to support his claim. "He is a perfect gentleman, a soul of honour," Sherring said. Unfortunately, this story was not widely circulated, and there are still people today who believe they were panhandled by Tom Longboat.

Early in 1949 Longboat came down with pneumonia. He died on January 9 at the age of sixty-one. Although he had been baptized so he could marry in a church, he had kept to the longhouse religion all his life. His god was still the Great Spirit, and he was buried according to the traditional faith. He was dressed in new cotton and wool that had been hand-stitched by the women in his family. His two white-fringed shirts and dark blue beaded trousers represented the colours of his tribe. A blue silk ribbon was tied across his chest, a shawl of the same material was draped over his shoulders, and a silk bandanna tied around his head. On his feet were new buckskin moccasins. A friend whittled a V in the top of the coffin to permit his spirit to escape. The entire service was spoken in Onondaga, the chants led by his two sons. Many people from the sports world were also in attendance, including Bill Sherring, Jim Corkery, Sol Mintz and Bobby Kerr, whose 1908 Olympic championship had been eclipsed in the public eye by the excitement surrounding Longboat's marathon.

Tom Longboat at 50

Tom Longboat was one of the greatest athletes Canada has ever seen. As an amateur, he lost only three races, including his first race at Caledonia. At the end of his brief amateur career he held two national track records and several unofficial world bests on the road. He held pro records for fifteen and twenty miles [24 & 32 km] and once came within seconds of breaking Deerfoot's record for twelve miles [19 km]. No other runner ever won three indoor marathons in less than two months. Even when he lost, Longboat was a courageous competitor, never giving up without a ferocious struggle.

At his death Alfie Shrubb told an interviewer, "... he was one of the greatest, if not the greatest marathoner of all time." More Canadians watched him perform than any other athlete in his generation. At his funeral Chief Leonard Staats said that "his athletic prowess was only surpassed by his qualities as a gentleman. He was liked by everyone." He rarely got angry, and when he did he usually kept silent. Perhaps he should have been more outspoken about the insults he received and the

TOM LONGBOAT
1886 - 1949

Near here was born one of the greatest marathon runners of all time, Tom Longboat, an Onondaga from the Grand River Reservation of the Six Nations Iroquois. From 1906 to 1912 he defeated most of the world's leading amateurs and professionals at distances of 12 to 26 miles. Longboat won the Boston Marathon, represented Canada in the 1908 Olympic games, and served overseas with the Sportsmen's Battalion and the Canadian Engineers 1916-1919

Erected by the Ontario Archaeological and Historic Sites Board

Historical plaque near his birthplace honouring Tom Longboat's accomplishments

promoters who exploited him. Frank Montour, a lifelong friend, suggested, "sometimes he was his own worst enemy; he was generous to a fault."

Since Longboat's day very few Canadian Aboriginals have excelled on the national sports scene. Albert Smoke of the Curve Lake Reserve near Peterborough competed in the 1920 Olympics, but no Aboriginal has made it to a national team since. George Armstrong, Jim Nielson, Reg Leach and Stan Jonathon, all of Aboriginal parentage, have competed successfully in the National Hockey League, but none has achieved the spectacular record of Longboat or some of the nineteenth-century Aboriginal champions.

The demise of Aboriginal athletes can only be explained in the context of the demise of Aboriginal communities across Canada. After World War I many bands entered a period of gradual economic decline from which they have never recovered. According to anthropologist Rolf Knight:

> *The 1930s were a watershed in native Indian labour history. Many of the previous kinds of Indian employment came to an end or were permanently reduced ... Although the collapse of small-scale enterprises was a process general throughout the Canadian economy during those years, it seems to have been of exceptional intensity among Indian-owned enterprises, and relatively few reappeared after the end of the depression.*

"A Perfect Gentleman"

Under these circumstances, many Aboriginals returned to their reserves to take up the subsistence farming, hunting, fishing and craft production that had not been widely practised for many years. But in most cases this was not enough to live on, and the government had to step in with welfare payments. Increasing poverty and despair sometimes turned slurs against Aboriginals into self-fulfilling prophecies.

Today, excellence in sport is largely determined by income and circumstance. Athletes who represent their provinces at the Canada Games or are successful enough to earn an Olympic berth are increasingly from upper middle-class urban families. A 1996 survey of high-performance amateur athletes found that the average personal income was under $20,000, about half the national average and very close to the poverty line. Success is also a function of regional wealth, for the construction of facilities usually requires community or government funds. Marginal non-Aboriginals as well as marginal Aboriginal communities have found it difficult to give their most promising athletes the resources they need.

But if there is any doubt that Aboriginal athletes could, in the proper circumstances, still make it to the top, the careers of Tom Longboat—or Joe Keeper, Jim Thorpe, Deerfoot or any one of hundreds of other Aboriginal athletes of years ago— should put the argument to rest. They were magnificent champions, and people who saw them were thrilled they were alive.

Tom Longboat

1887	Tom Longboat is born on June 4 in Ohsweken, Ontario
1899	Enrolls in the Mohawk Institute but runs away soon after
1905	Enters Victoria Day race and comes in second
1906	Enters Hamilton *Herald*, Ward Marathon and Christmas Day races and wins all three
1907	Enters Boston Marathon and wins, breaking the record by five minutes
	Wins several races as member of Irish Canadian Athletic Club (ICAC)
1908	Takes part in 1908 Olympic Marathon but collapses after 32 km
	Turns professional; beats Dorando Pietri in an indoor marathon in New York
	Marries Lauretta Maracle on December 28
1909	Races Alf Shrubb at Madison Square Garden and beats him
1911	Receives suspended sentence for drunkenness, fuelling alcoholism myth
1912	Turns in his fastest time ever for 24 km race in Scotland
1914	World War I begins in Europe
1916	Volunteers for military service
	Continues racing competitively for various regiments
	Serves as a dispatch runner in France and is wounded twice
1919	Demobilized and wins race against Bill Queal of New York
c 1920	Marries Martha Silversmith and they have four children
1926	Finds permanent job with Toronto streets department as a garbageman
1927	Wins a second-hand car in a race celebrating Hamilton's Diamond Jubilee
1930	His 8-year-old daughter is killed by a car
1945	Retires to a small house on Six Nations Reserve in Brantford; continues walking long distances
1946	Hospitalized with diabetes
1947	Gives newspaper interview to correct errors about his alleged alcoholism
1949	Dies from pneumonia on January 9

Further Reading

Adams, Howard. *Prison of Grass.* Toronto: General, 1977.

Batten, Jack. *The Man Who Ran Faster Than Everyone: the story of Tom Longboat.* Toronto: Tundra Books, 2002.

Cosentino, Frank and Glynn Leyshon. *Olympic Gold: Canada's Winners in the Summer Games.* Toronto: Holt, Rinehart and Winston, 1975.

Killanin, Lord and John Rodda. *The Olympic Games.* New York: Collier-Macmillan, 1976.

Knight, Rolf. *Indians at Work.* Vancouver: New Star, 1978.

Lovesey, Peter. *The Kings of Distance.* London: Eyre and Spottiswoode, 1968.

North American Indian Travelling College. *Tewaarathon (Lacrosse) Akwesasne's Story of Our National Game.* St. Regis, P.Q.: NAITC, 1978.

Patterson, E. Palmer. *The Canadian Indian, a History Since 1500.* Toronto: Collier-Macmillan, 1972.

Credits

The publisher wishes to thank the following for their generous assistance: the Longboat family, Bill Dunning, Willie Littlechild, John Smart, Canada's Sports Hall of Fame, City of Toronto Archives, Kanawa International Museum of Canoes and Kayaks, Public Archives of Canada and the Woodland Indian Cultural and Educational Centre.

The publishers wish to express their gratitude to the following who have given permission to use copyrighted illustrations in this book:

Canada Archives, pages 11(PA-51882), 14(PA-050481), 17(C-014095), 20(PA-050294), 22(PA-049972), 27(PA-050414), 43(PA-049905), 51(C-029484), 53(PA-001479), 59(PA-050409)
City of Toronto Archives (James Collection), pages 33, 57
Cosentino, Frank and Glynn Leyshon, page 30
Hamilton Public Library, page 13
Hamilton *Spectator,* page 58
National Library of Canada, Toronto *Globe,* page 37(8209)
Ontario Archives, pages 5(S4013), 6(S4749), 7(S6977), 12(S898)
Sports Hall of Fame, Toronto, pages 24, 28, 35, 39, 40, 41, 46, 47, 49, 63

Every effort has been made to credit all sources correctly. The publishers will welcome any information that will allow them to correct any errors or omissions.

Index